THE ARISTOCRACY OF THE TAURUS MIND.... THE FIRST WONDER OF EXISTENCE!!!

Introduction

KRAYZIE BONE AKA LEATHERFACE AKA MR. SAWED OFF AKA PICASSO AKA BEAUTIFUL DARKNESS PARLAYS IN THE MIND AKA BEAUTIFUL LOTUS FLOWER AKA PURE SPIRIT IN RUTHLESS ENVIRONMENT.

WISH BONE AKA STRAIGHTJACKET AKA PAIN'S
COMPANION AKA MARTYR ON DUTY FOR HIS TRUES AKA
ASTRAL WONDERMENT AKA INNOCENT STARGAZER LILY
AKA MOST FRAGRANT SACRIFICIAL LAMB

BRYON ANTHONY McCANE II AKA BIZZY BONE AKA RIP AKA MOST RAREST FLOWER OF THEM ALL: SILVER LOTUS FLOWER AKA GROWS TO A MOST PURE DIVINE MATURITY BY MEANS OF REMOTE HARSH FROST OF THE WINTER IN ORDER TO GERMINATE

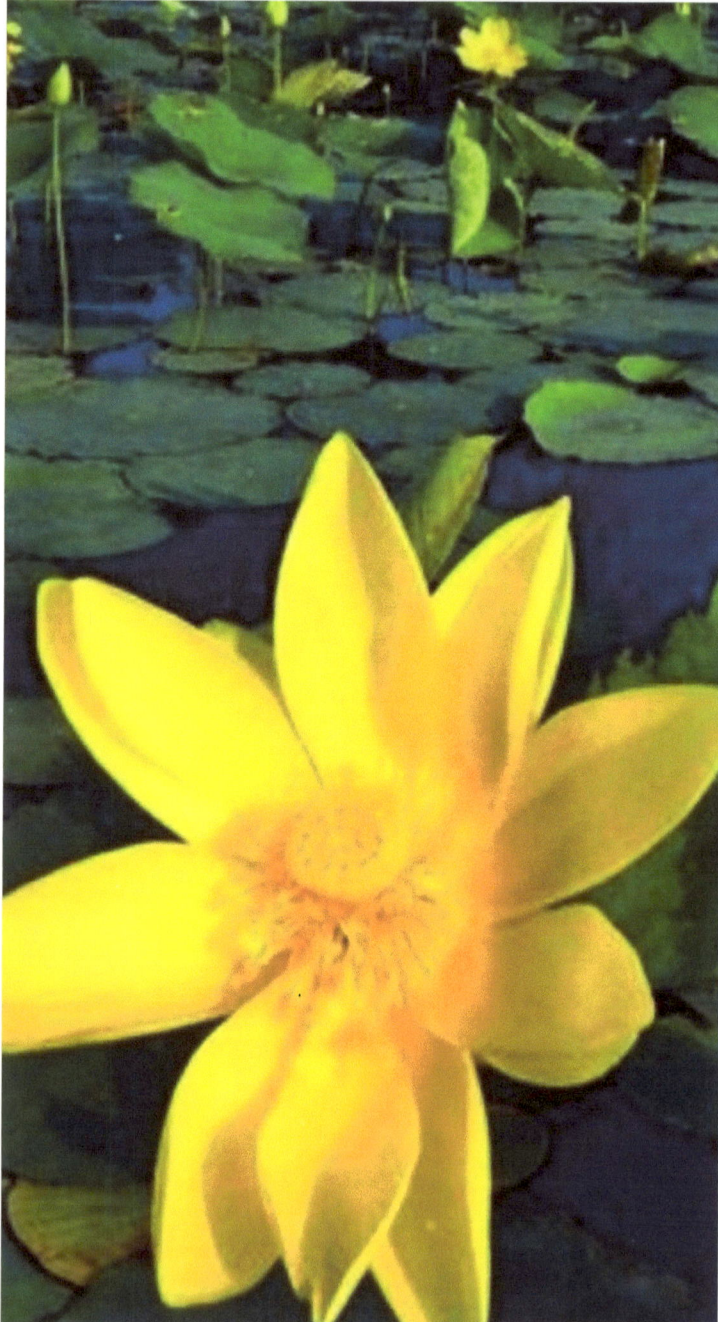

LAYZIE BONE AKA NUMBER ONE ASSASSIN AKA L BURNA AKA FUCK YOU AND YOURS AKA MIND, INTENT, AND ACTIONS OF A SOULJAH AKA BLACK OPULENT LILY AKA CALIBRATION TO THAT OF THE MOST SOVEREIGN AUTHORITY AND POWER

FLESH N BONE AKA MR. STANLEY HOWSE AKA PRIMITIVE WILDFLOWER AKA ELUSIVE ENIGMATIC DIVINITY

This Book Is Dedicated To The Muse's Incubator.

Prologue

This Book Is Meant To Be A Stimulant To All Geniuses, Musicians, Architects, And Mathematicians, Without You All The World ● As We Know It Wouldn't Exist. So On Behalf Of All Of The Grateful Ones For All That You Do And HAVE DONE In And To The World ● I Say Thank You, For All Of Your Tireless Efforts And Contributions That No-one Could Number. This Book Is A Small Long Overdue Token Of Appreciation. THANK YOU!!!

Book Anatomy

Chapter 1 The Anatomy And Physiology Of Music Exhibition

Everything that exists in a musical note is harmony…. There is no opposition. Yet a single musical note is the most complex and most involved substance in existence. Not to Mention a musical note is the exact embodiment of THE SOVEREIGN CELESTIAL ONE. It is not humans, or the elements, or plants, or animals, or the stars, or the planets that were made in HIS IMAGE…. No But it is Music And Music Alone that is and was made in GOD'S IMAGE.

Just like in a musical note there is harmony only, and no opposition, so it is what is contained Within GOD, and yet HE is the most complex, most involved individual that exists. Out of all of creation MUSIC IS GOD'S MOST BELOVED, AND IS ALSO HIS MOST BEAUTIFUL EXPRESSION.

A Heptatonic Scale melds into new life, completion, mysticism, elitism, aloofness, refinement, highness, moral selectism, and anarchic symphony.

Largely absent in the chronicles of the life of Christ is music. Music is found nowhere in what we are made to believe is the embodiment of Christ, or any religious leader for that matter. Music is the most beautiful expression of GOD'S creation, which leads me to believe that the real essence and embodiment of Christ Has been left out of history. I don't believe of all things that Christ would have chosen to be a carpenter or that He would have chosen to teach and lead through parables.

I instead believe that Christ Is and was the Ultimate Musician, and that when He was on this Earth in physical form that His profession was that of a Prolific Symphonic Composer of Funky Superlative Melodic Harmonious Anarchic Rock 🎸 With Jazz Undertones Laced With Erotic Provocative Cryptic Mystical Controversial Blount Lyrics That Were All Full Of Earthy Cosmic Heavenly Wonder.

I feel that the reason it's undocumented is because Christ's Musical Genius Was to the human mind & psyche unfathomable & incomprehensible, to enormous for life, leaving the task to great for anyone to be able to transcribe or to put into words resulting in a musicless almost inanimate Teacher Master and Lord transcribed down through the ages.

GOD made the insect, plant, animal, elemental, and human species. When HE was done HE SAW in all of these existed bleak life. Then GOD CREATED something called music and at music's conception GOD SAID TO HIMSELF THAT this substance is a unique, taboo, forbidden, erogenous, euphoria, and just as HE was about to banish it, HE NOTICED that it sparked implosive and explosive catalysts called antigens, endorphins, pheromones, and rapid fire 🔥 neurotransmitters

To instantaneously manifest throughout the insect, plant, animal, elemental, and human phenomena. Then GOD SAID EUREKA this music substance is vital to the viability of MY creation. And so THE SOVEREIGN CELESTIAL DIVINE ONE saturated the cosmos, stars and planets with this raw, rarest, most tangible substance. Everything down to the most simplest form of matter pulsates within and without with the symphonic harmony that is music ♪♪.

Music is astute. Music is astral Wonderment. Music is Astronomical. Music is Astounding.

Music leaves one Breathless. A Single musical masterpiece is a plethoral bounty. Music lays bare all leaving many naked in its wake and nothing is left to desire of the imagination. Music is blatantly brutal it unmasks fraudulent communal facades.

Music is clever. Music is coy. Music is not colorblind. In Pre And Post timelessness music is completion and for those that are and have been encapsulated in the realm of time, music is perceived as controversial.

Music is demure in the company of wickedness. It does not lend its refinement in the presence of low class. Music is as dazzling as a fresh winter bed of snow ❄. Music is as dashing as a Prince Charming rescuing a damsel in distress. Music is as debonair and dapper as Prince Rogers Nelson When He puts on His Royal diggs (Which basically anything He decides to wear He Freaks It).

Music is elusive. Music is the Ether. Music is enigmatic. Music is ecstasy.

Music is furtive in the fact that the creating of it is not easily accessible. Music finesses the most impenetrable and most gullible of souls. Before you know it despite all of your resistance to it, you're enraptured with all of its flair and its shrewd mystical Devil Take It Adventure. Music is fantastical Wizardry, it purposely haphazardly mesmerizes.

Music is the furrow needed to uproot the souls that are weeds in the soil of life, in order to distinguish, plant, and set apart souls that are seeds that will bloom into the most bountiful healthy crops to ever exist.

Music is GOD'S most gallant soldier, always ready and willing to stand on the front lines in the face of adversity, terror, and danger. Music is Gasoline ready to douse the flames to set hell ablaze for all eternity. Music is so lethal that all it needs is to be gaunt to swallow up the girth of wickedness, much in the same way that a seemingly gaunt serpent opens his mouth to swallow a camel.

Music is an eternal graveyard. It's where everything goes to die and get sifted to determine who will stay in the eternal graveyard and who will rise to everlasting life. Music is a G, can't nobody fuck wit it, cause if you do it will consume you and all that will be left of you is the distant fumes of your memory.

To every addict when it comes to your sobriety, music will make you fall off the wagon because it gets you high, higher than the sun ✹, the moon ☾, and the stars ✸, and you can forget about ever coming back down. Instead of Temples constructed from the hands of filthy men that are filled with evil schemes and wicked hidden agendas, Rather GOD CHOOSES to dwell in the etheric halidom ruins that is Music. In the celestial realm Music is heralded from the valley of galaxies.

The stages that Music produces throughout the millennia of time are Herms for seers to know how close or how far time is from the final curtain being drawn on this temporal Final Act in the stage play called life that everyone in the earthly plane has starred in, and then comes The Coup De Grace. The Final Judgement. There will be no applause or requests for an encore.

Music does not put up facades. Its Incivility is laid bare for all to hear, and feel, and whether it's received jovially or reticent is of no consequence. Although Music is and has been Blatantly Blount and has held no reservations about its precision & straightforwardness it has been ineffectual ie failed to bring what would eventually be every humans desired awakening to rigid sensibility purity and compassion, after their actuation of their Eternal Destiny.

Music's Indomitability has weakened, subdued, and confined all under and to its service whether one is used to compose it or one is left devoid of being able to compose or enjoy it than that one is lured to and lulled by the capital to be gained by the exploitation of music and the vessels it chooses to manifest itself through. And the one or ones become salacious over the discovery of their own uncanny ability to be SLIME BUCKETS,

By Defrauding And weaving intricate webs of manipulation. So whether for good or bad Music has got you within its grasp and it will expose your epicenter whether your core is pure and undefiled or whether its consumed with maggots, flies, and decay.

Jimi Hendrix, Miles Davis, James Brown, Larry Graham, Prince Rogers Nelson's Jam Session ✎ will be the acid jazz (FUNK) that will be the backdrop sounds of the FINAL JUDGMENT. MUSIC SELECTS JUGGERNAUTS to produce and compose ITS MOST WORTHY VALUABLE AUTHENTICITY. BY JOVE ITS MUSC'S MOST PRECIOUS JEWEL....FUNK!

A jughead is MUSIC'S. MUSIC PERFORMS reverse psychology on jugheads by making them think that they have musical chops and musical inclinations and it makes them produce superficial synthetic,mediocrity that lulls the masses to deeper levels of sedative stupor-like Haziness. This way MUSIC INSURES THE ETERNAL FATE OF THOSE THAT SIT ON THE SIDELINES IN silence AND inactivity WHILE INJUSTICE RUNS RAMPANT!!!

Music is the kenotic Member of the Trinity Forever encased in leather filled with entrails. Music is the only kerygma that was ever needed to bring about awareness of GOD, christ, and HIS angel. Music is kinetic art with varying degrees of exquisite beauty and dark tempests The two are interchangeable because from the depths of the deepest darkest Tempests Emerges The Most Exquisite Beauty: The Black Race! Music Is KIN To The Black Race!

The last rites in the resurrection of the wicked will be chosen for them. Their last rites will be that the haze will be removed from their eyes and the reality of music will be revealed to them, Which will be the beginning of their TERROR When they finally awaken to what has eluded them in plain sight or rather plain hearing.

Afterward there will be a lush appetizing feast at the lord's table.

Music is of the same calibration as latitude, and had as much deference of the longitude of the highest celestial height descending into the deepest darkest celestial abyss.

To many music is deemed nugatory and to those who deem it so they themselves are an insignificant needle in the ions of haystacks in eternity. And to the few precious souls who deem music as necessitate are the bowels in the fulfillment of eternity.

Chapter 2 The Complex Simplicity Of Geometry

Everything wishes to be profound. Yet it's the simple conquests and the elementary things in life and in the universe that matter. A simple conquest ie true self discovery. An elementary thing in life ie organic raw materials vital to survival like water, vegetation, and cotton with which to be clothed(A SEAMSTRESS AND A TAILOR IS THE MOST DELICATE AND MOST IMPORTANT OF ALL ARCHITECTS). An elementary thing in the universe is not an atom, or a proton, or an electron, or a neutron, on the contrary it's the celestial movement of the planets, sun, moon, & stars, that keep us warm, balanced and is our divine guidance for

The course of our everyday actions,decisions, and movements.

There are two spheres of geometry, one is an oxymoronic wonder and that is geometry that's of inanimate physiology such as a building constructed out of shapes made of stone, marble, glass, etc. It's inanimate because it does not have autonomous movement and its physiology is that buildings serve as a function to shelter life among other things.

And the most oxymoronic wonder of of all and that is that solid shapes that are also malleable & fluid at the same time which are natural structures that are really supernatural anarchic yet organized shapes and structures such as clothes, the human body, plants, flowers 🦃, animals and birds 🐦 of every kind.

Chapter 3 The Auric Energy Field Of Numbers

Born out of the numbers nine and eight is among other things the mystical number seven. When nine the number of perfection and eight the number that brings forth new age, and new life, and latter new beginning were meshed together in a colorful symphony of complexity. Seven was born which is the number of latter creation, latter creativity, and Intuitive Clarity of Unspeakable Proportions, SEVEN IS THE NUMBER THAT IS THE ONE AND ONLY MUSE THAT FURTIVELY FORE INSPIRED

THE LATTER CREATION.

In short music is the number 9 and the number 9 is music because 9 is the number of perfection and music is perfection. The Number 9 is married to the number SEVEN because SEVEN is the number of Completion and once 9 or perfection or music was born Seven or completion automatically existed because the number 9 perfection made NUMBER SEVEN OR COMPLETION THUS YOU HAVE THE FIRST MARRIAGE 9 AND SEVEN. SEVEN IS 9's FLOATING RIB!.